TEACHER'S PACK

Speaking of Values 2

Conversation and Listening

Robin Mills

PEARSON
Longman

Speaking of Values 2: Conversation and Listening
Teacher's Pack

Pearson Education, 10 Bank Street, White Plains, NY 10606

Staff credits: The people who made up the *Speaking of Values 2 Teacher's Pack* team, representing editorial, production, design, and manufacturing, are: Danielle Belfiore, Christine Edmonds, Laura Le Dréan, Amy McCormick, Martha McGaughey, Shana McGuire, Joan Poole, Edith Pullman, and Patricia Wosczyk.

Cover design: Patricia Wosczyk
Text design: Patricia Wosczyk
Text composition: Laserwords
Text font: Minion

ISBN: 0-13-195661-2

LONGMAN ON THE **WEB**

Longman.com offers online resources for teachers and students. Access our Companion Websites, our online catalog, and our local offices around the world.

Visit us at **longman.com.**

Printed in the United States of America
5 6 7 8 9 10–OPM–09 08

CONTENTS

INTRODUCTION

The material in this Teacher's Pack is provided to help you, the teacher, meet the needs of your students. It includes suggestions for using the student book, the photocopiable unit quizzes and their answer keys, the student book answer key, and the audioscripts for the Listening sections in the student book.

TEACHING SUGGESTIONS

Most of us who teach today see a textbook as a guidebook rather than a recipe book. The needs and interests of a particular class help us to decide how we're going to use the material in a book. The following suggestions will help you get the most out of the material in *Speaking of Values 2* as you take into consideration the needs and interests of your students.

THINKING ABOUT THE TOPIC

The illustration or photo can be used in a variety of ways.

- Have students work in groups to look at the picture and write down all the things they can name. You may need to help students with unfamiliar or technical vocabulary. For example, in Unit 11: Is It the Best Medicine? you may want to describe some of the medical procedures that students may not be familiar with.
- Have a student from each group write the words on the board. This exercise helps students remember words they've learned, involves them in the subject, and allows you to introduce new words.
- Have students write *Wh-* questions (*who, what, where, why, how*) about the illustration or photo. For example, in Unit 5: Is *That* Entertainment? they might write: *Where are the people in each picture? How old are they? What are they doing? What are they wearing? What are their occupations? How do they feel?* After writing the questions, the students can answer them (in writing or orally) in their groups, switch lists with another group and answer them, write them on the board for the class to answer, or take them home to answer for homework. The same activities can be done orally.
- Have students categorize vocabulary. For example, in Unit 1: Is Your Privacy Really Private? students can list words for emotions. In Unit 4: Why Blow the Whistle? students can list verbs.

TALKING ABOUT YOUR EXPERIENCE

In this section, students work with a partner or a group to talk about their own life experiences. For example, in Unit 2: Is Winning Everything? students react to the use of performance-enhancing drugs and discuss their opinions on the subject. Exploring their own opinions helps them prepare for the listening activity.

Check to make sure students understand each question before they answer it. As they are working together, circulate in the classroom so that you can spend time with quiet or less advanced students.

After students have worked with a partner or in a group, you can do several things. One option is to choose a question that students have answered and ask several students for their answers. Another is to ask students to report anything interesting they've learned from their classmates. You also can assign one student to be the reporter for each group and to give a summary of the group's answers for the class. Have other groups add answers not given or have them agree/disagree and explain their positions.

Each group or pair-work activity is followed by questions that can be discussed with a partner, a small group, or the entire class. Let the students' reactions to the questions guide the discussion. Each pair, group, or class may find a different question most interesting to answer. For example, in Unit 8: How Important Are Family Ties? some students might enjoy talking about the different responses men and women have to the issue of adult children returning to their parents' house to live, and why. After students have worked in pairs or small groups, you can have them summarize their overall responses, describe a favorite question, or talk about which question generated the most discussion and why.

LISTENING

A master teacher once said, "Never waste a good listening." Here are some ways to get the most out of every listening:
- Photocopy the audioscript, but delete some words. Ask students to listen and complete the conversation.
- Photocopy the audioscript, deleting one of the speaker's lines or parts of one of the speaker's lines. Have students try to complete the conversation before they listen. After they listen, have them compare their answers with what they've heard.
- Have students orally summarize the listening and then write a short summary, either as a group in class or individually for homework. This can also be done as a jigsaw activity, as follows: Students work in groups. Each student takes one point of the listening and summarizes it. Other students in the group help the student fill in any details that might have been missed. Once everyone agrees on the details, each student writes a summary of the section they focused on, on a separate piece of paper. When everyone has finished a section, the group assembles the sections in order.
- Give students key phrases to start off a section of the listening and then have them continue in their own words. For example, in Unit 9: Information Technology—Pros and Cons, you might give the students the phrase, "I know you only want what is best for the kids but . . ."
- Have students take on the roles of the speakers and improvise a conversation. Encourage them to work more for fluency than for accuracy in this exercise. It will give them the feeling of speaking at length.
- Ask students to agree or disagree with the overall point or message of the listening, and explain their position.

WORDS AND PHRASES ABOUT THE TOPIC

When students say they "know" a word or phrase, they usually mean they understand it. In some instances, items in the Words and Phrases section include words that students will be able to understand and use. In other cases, students will be able to understand the vocabulary, but may not be able to use it yet. It is important for students to study both types of vocabulary items—ones they can use and ones they can understand but can't use yet. If vocabulary is limited only to words and phrases students can already use actively, they will not be prepared to understand and read at higher levels. If they focus only on the more difficult items, they will increase their comprehension, but not their active use of the vocabulary. Since not all students are at the same level, the receptive vocabulary for some will be the productive vocabulary for others.

You may wish to give your students a checklist like the following to reinforce the idea that merely understanding a word is not the final goal.

Word and Phrases Checklist

Word/Phrase _____

I understand the meaning.	☐
I can pronounce the word correctly.	☐
I know the parts of speech possible for the word.	☐
I can use the word correctly when I speak and write.	☐

The Words and Phrases section asks students to focus on lexical items that are related to the content of the unit. Each item should be practiced many times and reviewed to provide students reasonable opportunity to learn it.

- Students can make flashcards of the vocabulary words and phrases to study.
- Students can create a grid, where each column represents a part of speech (noun, verb, adjective, adverb). They then list the correct form (if any) for each word, and write their own original sentences with the words and phrases. Not all words and phrases will lend themselves to this. Students might like to keep a running list for the whole book. Following is an example from Unit 4: Why Blow the Whistle?

Vocabulary Word in Text	Noun	Verb	Adjective	Adverb
conscientious	conscientiousness	(none)	conscientious	conscientiously
Original Sentence: <u>A conscientious employee is likely to notice when something is being done improperly.</u>				

- Students can prepare quizzes for each other using the vocabulary from the unit. After you have checked and corrected these quizzes, they can be used to review the words and phrases.
- Students might also like to keep a running list of words that come up throughout each unit, in other exercises, or in the listening. They can use these words to do the above activities as well. Any vocabulary words that come up can be used for further practice.

PROBLEM SOLVING

This section remains the heart of the text. Students consider problems and are asked to come up with a solution and defend it. They then discuss the problems in small groups. No other type of activity develops critical thinking skills as successfully as values clarification exercises.

Different roles can be assigned to each student in a group. There can be a facilitator who ensures everyone gets a turn to talk, a note taker who takes notes on the decision-making process, a reporter who reports to the class, and a time keeper who keeps track of the time so that each person has time to speak and the group has time to get to each problem.

While students are working in groups, walk around and monitor the discussion in each group. First, listen to their discussion, asking for clarification and details as you need them. After you have heard each group, you will be able to lead a more interesting follow-up discussion. For example, you might say, "It's interesting that two groups believe . . . while the other two groups believe just the opposite." Then have each group defend its belief. Help each group form better arguments. Point out contradictions. Give students time to organize and think through their ideas.

For variety, you might want to have each group choose only one problem to discuss, and then have them report to the class.

In this edition the problems and choices are recorded on the complete audio CD program. This offers the teacher more options in presenting the material.
- Students can listen with books closed.
- They can listen and read at the same time.
- They can listen and write the problem.
- They can listen to the problem and give an answer before hearing or reading the choices given in the text.

You might want to have the students role-play the problems as part of the problem-solving activity or as a follow-up activity.

FROM THE NEWS

Students read authentic, high-interest news articles taken from English language newspapers. The level of language is somewhat more difficult than in the rest of the text; this is because students often read at a higher level than they can speak or write. Students can reread the text and use a dictionary without the embarrassment that comes from not being able to express ideas on the spot orally.

The readings are recorded so that they can be used to give students additional opportunities to improve their listening comprehension skills. Opinion questions follow the readings to help develop students' critical thinking skills. These questions can also be the basis for a written activity.

Some options for teaching this section include the following:
- Ask students to read the articles before coming to class. Then they can listen in class to the article on the audio CD.
- Go over the warm-up question and the title. Have students make predictions about the reading based on the title.
- If the vocabulary is not clear from the context, go over any new words before students read the article.
- Have students summarize the news article orally and/or in writing.
- Have students read the first sentence of each paragraph and make predictions about the paragraph based on the first sentence.
- Assign one paragraph to each member of a group. Have students read silently and then summarize the paragraph orally for the whole group.
- Have students outline the reading in writing after they read the article.
- Have students give an oral or a written response to the reading. The response can be in support of or opposed to the view of the whole article or one particular point raised in the article. It can be something that surprised them, or a retelling of a similar experience of their own.
- Students can write a "letter to the editor" in response to an article.
- Any point raised in the reading can serve as a springboard to further research.

WORDS AND PHRASES FROM THE READING

The section called Words and Phrases from the Reading follows each reading. These exercises check students' understanding of phrases in the article. The Unit Quizzes test these particular vocabulary words and phrases and can be given any time after this point in the unit.

CONVERSATION TIP

This section provides phrases and expressions for students to use in the Act It Out role-play section. These functions, or social language, include ways of making suggestions, expressing preferences, agreeing or disagreeing, and asking for information. It's important for students to understand that learning these functions will help them become more fluent.

ACT IT OUT

In this section students do a role play. The situation is related to the unit theme, and it provides an opportunity to use the expressions in the Conversation Tip section. Some students will put on a show and enjoy pretending, while others may twist the situation around so that they speak as themselves. Either way of doing a role play can be valuable, as long as the students practice using the expressions in the Conversation Tip box.

How you listen to student performances depends on the number of students in your class. In small classes it may be possible for you to hear each group practice and then, after you've helped them, have them perform for the class. In larger classes, you might want to ask a few groups to perform for the class. You could also pair up groups and have them listen to each other. Here are some suggestions for role plays:

- As other students listen to role plays, assign listening tasks. For example, have students who are listening write down three points made by a speaker, or decide which person they agree with and why.
- Students who are listening can also use the time to develop note-taking skills by outlining what they hear or by taking short notes that they then use to write a summary of the role play.
- Students who are listening can be asked to do a quick oral summary of what the students in the role play said.
- Students can write down their role plays and then turn them in to you.

Note: In Unit 10: A Good Place to Work, be sure to point out that the informational interview is different from an actual interview. In an informational interview, one might ask about salary, but in an actual job interview, that question would not be asked until later in the process.

PROVERBS OR SAYINGS

Encourage students to give examples that show the meaning of the proverb or saying. Ask for their opinions and help them to clarify their ideas in English. You might want to have students share relevant proverbs they know from their own culture.

BEYOND THE CLASSROOM

You may not have enough time for each student to do a presentation. If you don't, students can give their presentations to small groups. Then as a midterm or final oral activity, let each student choose one presentation to give to the class.

It can be challenging for intermediate-level students to do oral presentations. However, if you help them, encourage them, inspire them, and get them to present for the class, they'll learn a great deal and feel proud of their work.

You can encourage students to practice at home. They can audiotape or videotape their presentation and then watch or listen to their own performance. Ask them to identify three things they did well (for example, pronunciation, content, demeanor) and three things they can improve.

UNIT QUIZZES

Name _____ Date _____

UNIT 1 QUIZ

Complete the conversations with words or phrases from the box. You might have to change the form of the word.

at your fingertips	automatically	consumer	edition
heads up	instantly	medication	scanner
track	zip on through		

1. A: I recently bought a new book but noticed it had originally been printed several years ago.

   B: You must have bought a second _____.

2. A: Most stores now have special machines that read a tag with information about the product, such as the price.

   B: Cashiers just need to run the product over a _____ to get that information.

3. A: I use a special electronic device that allows me to drive through toll gates without stopping to pay. It saves me a lot of time.

   B: Those electronic devices allow drivers to _____.

4. A: The software in my computer is updated whenever I sign on to the Internet. I don't have to do anything.

   B: The software is updated _____.

5. A: My computer is quite fast. Images appear on the screen very quickly.

   B: Images appear _____.

6. A: The Internet has made information available quickly and easily. You no longer need to go to the library to do research.

   B: The Internet has put information _____.

7. A: I appreciate people at work warning me when the boss is in a bad mood.

   B: It is nice to get a _____ about potential problems.

8. A: RFID tags are one way for manufacturers to follow their products once they leave the store.

   B: RFID tags allow manufacturers to _____ their products.

9. A: Doctors are able to give patients many drugs to help them when they are sick.

    B: Doctors can prescribe the proper _____ for the patient's problem.

10. A: My friend buys a lot of different beauty products.

    B: She is a _____ of beauty products.

Unit 2 Quiz

Complete the sentences with the words and phrases from the box. You might have to change the form of the word.

atmosphere	constructive	free market	gratification
integrity	scrutinized	self-imposed	shortsighted
shortcuts	weigh in on		

1. I handed my passport to the customs officer; he _____ it carefully to make sure it was mine.

2. In order to save time when commuting to work, I look for _____ rather than just going the usual way.

3. There is nothing like the _____ of doing something very well.

4. In a _____ economy, prices are not controlled by the government.

5. I think everyone in the group had something to say; they all _____ the topic.

6. My boss gives me helpful, insightful comments on my work. His feedback is very _____.

7. People who plan for the future are not _____.

8. I enjoy the casual _____ of an outdoor restaurant in the summer.

9. I respect people with _____. I believe honesty and high moral principles are important qualities.

10. Professional athletes have to have a certain amount of _____ discipline in order to succeed in their sport; no one can force them to work hard.

UNIT 3 QUIZ

Read the sentences. Circle the letter of the best definition for each underlined word or phrase.

1. When you enter a store, there are often large displays showing reduced prices on a variety of items. These displays are intended to show the customers what <u>deals</u> the store is offering.

    a. leftover items still available for sale

    b. agreements or arrangements, especially in business, such as good prices

2. Stores will often print coupons in the local newspaper to get more customers into the store. This is one way to <u>increase</u> sales.

    a. make larger

    b. make more efficient

3. <u>Normally</u> I like to visit with friends in the evenings and on the weekend, but sometimes I'll just stay home alone and read a good book.

    a. sometimes, but very not often

    b. usually, under typical conditions

4. The report <u>indicates</u> that consumers prefer to buy some merchandise, such as paper towels, in larger packages.

    a. shows

    b. proves

5. When my sister got married, an announcement was <u>published</u> in the local newspaper.

    a. added to the newspaper as a separate piece of paper

    b. printed in the newspaper

6. Some people think they can <u>counteract</u> the effects of a bad diet by exercising, but in fact it is important both to eat well and to exercise.

    a. reduce or prevent the bad effect of something

    b. improve

7. I <u>conducted</u> several research projects while I was in graduate school.

    a. read

    b. did

8. My travels have <u>spanned</u> several continents and numerous countries.
   a. included
   b. excluded

9. Most people know about the harmful <u>effects</u> of smoking.
   a. consequences
   b. reputation

10. The shoes looked expensive, but they weren't, because they were <u>marked down</u>.
    a. cheaper than the original price
    b. worn out

UNIT 4 QUIZ

Complete the sentences with the words and phrases from the box. You might have to change the form of the word.

authorities	codes of professional ethics	deterioration	get the ax
get rid of	justified	retaliation	scandal
suppress	tolerate		

1. Doctors, lawyers, and other professionals are expected to follow

    _____.

2. I used to be very healthy, but lately I've noticed a _____ in my health. I seem to be sick all the time.

3. The manager tried to _____ several employees she felt were not doing a good job.

4. Some pharmaceutical companies have tried to _____ research findings that show dangerous side effects of some of their drugs.

5. Whistle-blowers always risk experiencing _____ such as being fired or having their work hours reduced.

6. Lazy or dishonest employees often _____.

7. The politician's career was ruined when he cheated on his taxes and the newspaper revealed the _____.

8. The employee felt her complaint was _____, so she took it to her supervisor.

9. In a multicultural society it is important to _____ everyone and not be judgmental or critical of anyone else's culture.

10. The _____ at the airport announced that a new security system had recently been installed.

UNIT 5 QUIZ

Read the sentences. Circle the letter of the best definition for each underlined word or phrase.

1. I had a few <u>mishaps</u> yesterday; I overslept, forgot my keys, and spilled coffee all over my clothes, but I had a good day at work anyway.

   a. problems resulting from carelessness

   b. small accidents or mistakes that do not have serious results

2. The newspaper is very successful. It has 2 million <u>subscribers</u>.

   a. people who read the newspaper

   b. people who pay money for a regular service

3. I recently <u>launched</u> a personal website where I advertise my business.

   a. started something new

   b. made a website which includes photographs

4. Last year there were several <u>natural disasters</u> such as earthquakes, tsunamis, and tornadoes.

   a. incidents caused by violent weather conditions

   b. sudden events, not man-made, that cause great damage or suffering

5. The advertiser <u>claims</u> the product will clean anything, but I won't believe it until I see it.

   a. states that something is true even though it has not been proven

   b. believes that something is true even though it has not been proven

6. Obesity has become <u>endemic</u> among teenagers.

   a. a new health problem

   b. always present in a particular place, or among a particular group of people

7. I heard an <u>inspiring</u> lecture the other day on choosing a career.

   a. giving people a small sense of interest

   b. giving people a desire to do something

8. For some reason, people often like to <u>peer</u> at accidents on the freeway. I just drive by without looking.

   a. to look very carefully or hard, especially because you cannot see something well

   b. look quickly and then look away

9. I really enjoy reading fiction. Nonfiction does not have the same <u>appeal</u> to me.

   a. a quality that makes someone or something attractive or interesting

   b. a quality that makes something irresistible to you even if you think it might not be good for you

10. There were 3,000 <u>spectators</u> at the auditorium.

   a. people who were watching

   b. people who were listening

UNIT 6 QUIZ

Complete the sentences with the words and phrases from the box. You might have to change the form of the word.

conjure up	dress down	dress up	institute
mandatory	perpetrate	resentful	restrictive
trendy	thrive on		

1. The smell of Thai food _____ fond memories of my travels in Thailand.

2. Most people in the financial industry have to _____ for work.

3. I _____ expressing myself through the clothes I wear. It really makes me happy.

4. My workplace has recently _____ a policy that allows employees to dress casually on Friday.

5. She always buys the latest fashions; her clothes are very _____.

6. On casual Fridays, everyone in my office _____. No one wears a suit or a tie.

7. My school has _____ testing in order to graduate. No one will receive a diploma without first passing the exam.

8. The man who _____ the crime was brought to trial.

9. Rules can take away people's ability to make decisions on their own, and if there are too many rules, the situation becomes _____.

10. If everyone in a group participates in making a decision, no one feels _____ because everyone has had a say in the outcome.

UNIT 7 QUIZ

Complete the conversations with words or phrases from the box. You might have to change the form of the word.

astute	emigrants	entrepreneurial	innovation
pioneer	proportion	remnant	stingy
sector	set aside		

1. A: I am impressed with people who can start a business by themselves, who are willing to take a risk to earn a profit.

    B: People who can do that are very _____.

2. A: It's so convenient that almost everyone has a computer at home these days. How did we ever manage before?

    B: Yes, whoever _____ the idea of home computers was really thinking ahead.

3. A: I enjoy reading the business section of the newspaper, especially the articles that talk about new machines and developments.

    B: Yes, it's always interesting to read about _____.

4. A: My father has the ability to understand business situations very well. That is why he has been successful.

    B: He is very _____.

5. A: When people leave their own countries in order to have a better life in another place, their children sometimes lose interest in the parents' culture and language.

    B: I think that is a common experience for _____.

6. A: What industries are you thinking of working in?

    B: I'd like a job in the business or insurance _____.

7. A: So many places in California have Spanish names!

    B: Yes, those are a _____ of the time when California belonged to Spain.

8. A: Do you think most rich people inherit their wealth?

    B: I think that a larger _____ inherits it than earns it.

9. A: Are your parents worried about their retirement?

    B: No, they've always saved their money, and they've _____ a nice nest egg.

10. A: He never offers to pay for anything! It makes me so mad.

    B: He's just _____. You can't change him.

UNIT 8 QUIZ

Read the sentences. Circle the letter of the best definition for each underlined word or phrase.

1. They decided not to travel to the island because of reports of <u>turmoil</u> there.
   a. too many people
   b. trouble

2. I think I have the <u>potential</u> to go to graduate school, but I am just not sure I want to.
   a. financial means
   b. ability

3. My sister and I share many <u>traits,</u> but we are different in many ways as well.
   a. things a person likes or enjoys doing
   b. particular qualities in someone's character or personality

4. He smoked for years, to the <u>detriment</u> of his health.
   a. bad effect
   b. ignoring something

5. Doctors are usually considered to have a high <u>status</u> in society.
   a. a person's social or professional rank or position
   b. amount of money a person has

6. The quality of restaurants in New York <u>runs the gamut</u> from fantastic to terrible.
   a. tends to be
   b. varies

7. We have <u>tentative</u> plans to go to Europe next year.
   a. not definite or certain
   b. definite or certain

8. Her pets are better <u>nurtured</u> than her children!
   a. in a good mood, happy
   b. well cared for

9. Children are more <u>resilient</u> than adults.

    a. able to quickly become strong, healthy, or happy again after an illness, difficult situation, or change

    b. young, full of energy, strong, and healthy

10. Some people really enjoy <u>domestic</u> work.

    a. in the home

    b. peaceful, not warlike

UNIT 9 QUIZ

Complete the sentences with words and phrases from the box. You might have to change the form of the word.

alleviate	be hard pressed	enlisted	enthusiast
genealogy	hit it off	isolation	pursuit
take to	virtual		

1. I am very curious about my family's history. I plan to take a class on _____ to help me do research.

2. My friend just started college. She has met some nice people she likes and now has a new group of friends. I am glad she has _____ with some people.

3. Computer technology has changed so much over the last few years. It is amazing what kinds of things can be made _____ now.

4. Bill and Jane just started ballroom dancing last year. They really _____ it; in fact, they won a competition last week.

5. A history _____ knows a lot about world events from the past.

6. People often take aspirin to _____ the pain of a headache.

7. You'd _____ to find someone who doesn't have a cell phone in New York these days. Everyone seems to have one.

8. Often people who spend too much time alone feel a sense of _____.

9. One neighbor on my street has _____ several of us to help make the street more beautiful by planting trees and flowers. We were happy to help.

10. My hobbies include hiking, swimming, and gardening but my favorite _____ is reading.

Unit 10 Quiz

Read the sentences. Circle the letter of the best definition for each underlined word or phrase.

1. His <u>gross</u> income was over $10 million last year! Isn't that incredible?
   a. before taxes
   b. very big

2. Many political problems <u>originate</u> in cultural differences.
   a. are explained by
   b. begin in

3. A great politician always has a <u>vision</u> for his or her country.
   a. an idea of what you would like to happen in the future
   b. a clear picture of reality

4. My mother is an <u>executive</u> in a large company.
   a. someone who manages others in an organization and helps decide what the organization will do
   b. one of the owners of a company

5. I have been a <u>shareholder</u> in a large Internet company for several years.
   a. someone who works for a company
   b. someone who owns stock in a business

6. I want to work in a place that has a lot of <u>collegiality</u>.
   a. equally shared power and authority among people
   b. quality of being well educated

7. With so many business scandals in the news lately, you have to wonder about some people's <u>ethical conduct</u>.
   a. morally good or correct behavior
   b. ability to be discreet, to keep a secret when necessary

8. I <u>guarantee</u> that the work will be finished by Wednesday.
   a. emphasize or stress something is true
   b. promise

9. Nowadays, many <u>operations</u> are worldwide, rather than carried out in only one country.

   a. businesses, companies, or organizations

   b. surgeries or other medical procedures

10. People have many different <u>motives</u> for doing volunteer work.

    a. reasons

    b. benefits

UNIT 11 QUIZ

Complete the sentences with words and phrases from the box. You might have to change the form of the word.

coercion	deficiencies	dilemma	diminish
elective	inevitable	momentum	prescription
reflexes	symptoms		

1. There are many medical procedures available now that are not necessary, such as plastic surgery for cosmetic reasons only. These are called _____ surgeries.

2. Two of my close friends are having their weddings on the same day. I can't go to both weddings, but I really don't want to hurt anyone's feelings. I don't know what to do; it's a real _____.

3. When a doctor uses a special instrument to hit below a patient's knee, she is testing the patient's _____.

4. Certain health problems are a direct result of vitamin _____.

5. He really loved the class at first, but as the work got harder, his enthusiasm

    _____.

6. Some minor problems are _____ whenever you start using a new computer program.

7. We've made a great start on this project! Let's keep working hard so that we don't lose our _____.

8. Most people do not like being forced to do something. _____ is not an effective way to get people's cooperation.

9. You need a _____ from a doctor before you can get most medicines from a pharmacy.

10. She has all the _____ of the flu: fever, chills, headache, runny nose, and joint pain.

UNIT 12 QUIZ

Complete the sentences with the expressions with run *from the box. You might have to change the form of the word. Be careful! One expression is used twice.*

run across	run after	run-down
run errands	run in	run out of
run through	run up	run up against

1. He has to be careful not to eat too much sugar, because diabetes _____ his family.

2. Don't forget to go to the gas station. You don't want to _____ gas.

3. I'd been looking everywhere for a blue suitcase, and I thought I'd never find one. Then I _____ one at the open-air flea market near my house.

4. Most musicians want to _____ their pieces at least once right before a performance.

5. On Saturday, first I went to the supermarket, then to the dry cleaners, then to the video store . . . I spent the whole day _____. I was exhausted!

6. You should never _____ a moving train. It's too dangerous.

7. It's easy to _____ a big credit card bill when you're on vacation.

8. He was really well prepared for the meeting. He _____ his presentation at least 10 times before the big day.

9. No one wants to live in an old _____ building.

10. The builders wanted to take out the park and put up a big building in the same place, but they _____ too much opposition from the local residents, so they had to find another place to build.

ANSWER KEY FOR UNIT QUIZZES

UNIT 1 QUIZ

1. edition   2. scanner   3. zip on through
4. automatically   5. instantly   6. at your fingertips
7. heads up   8. track   9. medication
10. consumer

UNIT 2 QUIZ

1. scrutinized   2. shortcuts   3. gratification
4. free market   5. weighed in on   6. constructive
7. shortsighted   8. atmosphere   9. integrity
10. self-imposed

UNIT 3 QUIZ

1. b   2. a   3. b   4. a   5. b   6. a   7. b   8. a
9. a   10. a

UNIT 4 QUIZ

1. codes of professional ethics   2. deterioration
3. get rid of   4. suppress   5. retaliation
6. get the axe   7. scandal   8. justified
9. tolerate   10. authorities

UNIT 5 QUIZ

1. b   2. b   3. a   4. b   5. a   6. b   7. b   8. a
9. a   10. a

UNIT 6 QUIZ

1. conjures up   2. dress up   3. thrive on
4. instituted   5. trendy   6. dresses down
7. mandatory   8. perpetrated   9. restrictive
10. resentful

UNIT 7 QUIZ

1. entrepreneurial   2. pioneered   3. innovations
4. astute   5. emigrants   6. sector   7. remnant
8. proportion   9. set aside   10. stingy

UNIT 8 QUIZ

1. b   2. b   3. b   4. a   5. a   6. b   7. a   8. b
9. a   10. a

UNIT 9 QUIZ

1. genealogy   2. hit it off   3. virtual   4. took to
5. enthusiast   6. alleviate   7. be hard pressed
8. isolation   9. enlisted   10. pursuit

UNIT 10 QUIZ

1. a   2. b   3. a   4. a   5. b   6. a   7. a   8. b
9. a   10. a

UNIT 11 QUIZ

1. elective   2. dilemma   3. reflexes
4. deficiencies   5. diminished   6. inevitable
7. momentum   8. coercion   9. prescription
10. symptoms

UNIT 12 QUIZ

1. runs in   2. run out of   3. ran across
4. run through   5. running errands   6. run after
7. run up   8. ran through   9. run-down
10. ran up against

STUDENT BOOK ANSWER KEY

UNIT 1

Listening (page 3)
1. a 2. b 3. b 4. a 5. b

Words and Phrases About Privacy (page 4)
1. infringe on 2. eavesdrop 3. reluctant
4. intimacy 5. confidential 6. classified

1. c 2. e 3. d 4. b 5. a

(page 5)
1. A: infringe on
   B: intimacy
2. B: reluctant
3. A: confidential
   B: none of your business
4. A: keep it to yourself
   B: eavesdropping
5. B: behind closed doors
6. A: hush-hush
   B: classified
7. B: invasion of privacy

From the News (page 8)
1. T 2. F 3. F 4. F 5. T 6. F

Words and Phrases from the Reading (page 9)
1. f 2. h 3. i 4. a 5. c
6. j 7. e 8. b 9. d 10. g

1. zip on through
2. at your fingertips
3. heads up

Suffixes (page 10)
1. invasion/invaded 2. track/tracking
3. restrict/restriction 4. convenience/convenient
5. expectation/expects

UNIT 2

Listening (page 16)
1. She could have done better.
2. She should be proud. She can go to the championships.
3. Her times are better and she has more stamina. Today she is strong.
4. She still needs to be faster.
5. She wants to take a drug to help build her muscles and improve her speed.
6. No.
7. It helped her friend run faster and she had fewer aches and pains, and she could work out longer and race harder.
8. He says drugs are an artificial way to mask pain; she could hurt herself.
9. Being the fastest.
10. They're taking the drugs, and she can't compete with them.

Words and Phrases About Sports (page 17)
1. gifted 2. sacrifice 3. dedication
4. stamina 5. triumph 6. championship

1. a 2. b 3. b 4. a

(page 18)
1. good sport 2. stamina 3. dedication
4. triumph 5. wins by a narrow margin
6. gifted 7. sacrifice 8. the playing field is level
9. won hands down 10. championship

From the News (page 21)
1. Money and fame.
2. Greed and glory—they want to win.
3. (a) The baseball players association has not fully addressed the problem. (b) Owners are unable to properly discipline inappropriate drug use.
4. It's worth risking infamy and poor health to become famous by setting records.
5. Performance-enhancing drug abuse is wrong.
6. They should behave properly because integrity matters.

Words and Phrases from the Reading (page 23)

Across	Down
4. atmosphere	1. gratification
5. scrutinized	2. constructive
8. infamy	3. abuse
9. amoral	6. clamor
10. shortcuts	7. integrity

1. f 2. c 3. a 4. e 5. d 6. b

UNIT 3

Listening (page 29)

Speaker 1: It's easy; it's only 99 cents per song; copying music for free is illegal; he doesn't want to get sued; you are violating the rights of the artists and the companies; all the people involved need to make a living.

Speaker 2: There is so much available music for free; no one can catch you; people make their own copies to give to others all the time; music is overpriced; new bands get access to a larger audience; the Internet gives them publicity; the music industry has too much control over how people get music.

Words and Phrases About Shopping (page 29)

1. merchandise **2.** squander **3.** economize
4. know-how **5.** frugal **6.** extravagant

1. b **2.** d **3.** c **4.** e **5.** a

(page 30)

1. a steal **2.** extravagant **3.** window shopping
4. marked down **5.** frugal **6.** merchandise
7. economize **8.** know-how **9.** sell like hotcakes
10. squander

From the News (page 33)

1. Promotions affect how consumers make purchases.
2. (a) multi-unit pricing; (b) purchase limits; (c) suggestive selling
3. Write their purchase amounts on their shopping lists and stick to them.
4. They make the consumer buy the product more often.
5. They increase the amount of the sale for that visit.

Words and Phrases from the Reading (page 34)

1. i **2.** h **3.** c **4.** d **5.** b
6. e **7.** f **8.** a **9.** g **10.** j

1. words of wisdom **2.** stick to them
3. reference point

UNIT 4

Listening (page 39)

Order of steps: 1, 4, 5, 3, 2

Words and Phrases About Whistle-Blowers (page 40)

1. conscientious **2.** informers **3.** anonymous
4. consequences **5.** misconduct

1. e **2.** d **3.** f **4.** b **5.** c **6.** a

From the News (page 43)

1. Whistle-blowers suffer many consequences as a result of their actions.
2. 69 percent of people who reported wrongdoings to their supervisor were fired; 53 percent of those who blew the whistle reported deterioration in their family relations.
Total number interviewed: 300 interviews, 200 surveys
Other answers:
Percentage who were fired for reporting to someone else: 80
Percentage who became depressed: 84
Percentage who took action because of their value system: 79
Percentage who said they were trying to avoid blame for others' misconduct: 16

Words and Phrases from the Reading (page 44)

1. a **2.** a **3.** a **4.** b **5.** b
6. b **7.** a **8.** b **9.** a **10.** a

(page 45)

1. b **2.** a **3.** c

UNIT 5

Listening (page 50)

1. B **2.** B **3.** D **4.** A **5.** D
6. I **7.** I **8.** I **9.** S **10.** S **11.** S

Words and Phrases About Watching Others (page 51)

1. gawk **2.** voyeuristic **3.** rubbernecking
4. spectator **5.** glance

1. getting a kick out of **2.** catch a glimpse of
3. can't take their eyes off

From the News (page 54)

1. It is the attraction to tragedy.
2. More than 125 territories and 35 million subscribers
3. They have to be careful not to offend anybody.
4. It would not be acceptable there.
5. It is about real people risking their lives to save people.

Words and Phrases from the Reading (page 54)

1. b **2.** j **3.** a **4.** c **5.** h
6. g **7.** d **8.** i **9.** f **10.** e

Collocations (page 55)

1. a **2.** b **3.** a **4.** a

Unit 6

Listening (page 59)

1. F **2.** T **3.** F **4.** F **5.** F **6.** F **7.** T **8.** F

Words and Phrases About Personal Appearance (page 60)

1. chic **2.** demeanor **3.** cosmetics
4. trendy **5.** physical **6.** attire

1. e **2.** a **3.** d **4.** c **5.** b

From the News (page 63)

1. F **2.** T **3.** T **4.** T **5.** F

Words and Phrases from the Reading (page 64)

1. c **2.** a **3.** a **4.** b **5.** c
6. b **7.** a **8.** c **9.** c **10.** c

1. b **2.** a **3.** c

Unit 7

Listening (page 70)

1. b **2.** b **3.** b **4.** b **5.** a **6.** b
7. a **8.** b **9.** b **10.** b **11.** a

Words and Phrases About Money (page 72)

1. spendthrift **2.** nest egg **3.** stingy
4. means **5.** set aside **6.** hoard

1. c **2.** d **3.** a **4.** b

1. living the high life, stingy
2. set aside
3. A. means
   B. spare no expense
4. A. nest egg
   B. hoard

5. spendthrift
6. on a shoestring
7. a dime a dozen

From the News (page 76)

1. 538 billionaires in 46 countries
2. They inherit money or they make it.
3. United States: 40%
   France: 2/3 (66 2/3%)
   United Kingdom: 2/3 (66 2/3%)
   Canada: 50%
4. They are astute investors or they pioneered something new or were innovators.
5. Countries that have relatively open social structures and that accept rewarding enterprising behavior seem to produce more rich people.

Words and Phrases from the Reading (page 76)

1. f **2.** c **3.** g **4.** a **5.** b
6. i **7.** h **8.** e **9.** j **10.** d

(page 77)

1. a **2.** b **3.** b **4.** a

Unit 8

Listening (page 82)

1. He has decided to stay.
2. She is moving to the city.
3. She loves them but hasn't lived close to them in years.
4. They are very close and see each other often.
5. He could do so much more if he moved away. He is limiting himself. His life will be a dead end.
6. He is sad so many people have decided to move away. He doesn't want to see the area die out.

Words and Phrases About Families (page 82)

1. domestic **2.** patriarchal **3.** blood relation
4. ancestor **5.** matriarchal **6.** descendants

(page 83)

1. b **2.** d **3.** a **4.** c

From the News (page 87)

1. They have been on their own in the world for a period of time and they have decided to move home temporarily.
2. Parents should have a plan to avoid potential problems and ensure a smooth-running home.
3. Ground rules should include a tentative limit on the length of time the child can remain in the home. General items include financial contributions and household chores. Specific

items include rent, telephone, utilities, cleaning, errands, yard work.
4. Move them back to independence as soon as possible.

Words and Phrases from the Reading (page 88)

1. f 2. c 3. h 4. b 5. d
6. a 7. e 8. i 9. j 10. g

1. run the gamut 2. ground rules
3. lose sight of the fact 4. fall back into
5. open ended 6. pull together

UNIT 9

Listening (page 93)

Father's attitude toward technology:
　　Technology changes so fast.
　　Wants his kids to have the best technology.
　　It will make their lives easier.
　　They should have state-of-the-art technology.
　　Kids can interact with others in another part of the world.
　　Have to keep up to be competitive.

Mother's attitude toward technology:
　　Kids spend too much time on the computer, using cell phones, and watching DVDs.
　　There is a lack of social interaction.
　　Kids don't use full sentences in chat rooms; it's bad for their writing skills.
　　Kids can meet the wrong kind of people in chat rooms.
　　There is too much technology and information available.

Words and Phrases About Information Technology (page 93)

1. c 2. i 3. e 4. d 5. f 6. b
7. h 8. g 9. a 10. l 11. j 12. k

From the News (page 97)

1. It ranges from "just curious" with no computer background to full-fledged nerds who have many computers.
2. They have published newsletters and created greeting cards.
3. Every age group is represented, from people in their 50s to people in their 90s.
4. Elderhostel (travel), SeniorNet, Virtual University, "Electric Village" for local information.
5. They communicate with their children by e-mail.
6. They have been able to learn about the latest medical news.

Words and Phrases from the Reading (page 97)

1. i 2. e 3. b 4. f 5. a
6. j 7. c 8. d 9. g 10. h

(page 98)

1. a 2. a 3. b 4. a 5. b

UNIT 10

Listening (page 104)

1. F 2. F 3. F 4. T
5. T 6. T 7. T 8. F

Words and Phrases About Business (page 104)

1. c 2. e 3. b 4. d 5. a

(page 105)

1. mom-and-pop 2. multinational corporation
3. public company 4. cooperative 5. charitable foundation

1. c 2. e 3. b 4. a 5. d

From the News (page 108)

1. The entire day's gross sales were divided among its employees.
2. $118 million.
3. All suppliers had to guarantee that the wood did not originate in ancient forests.
4. Home furnishings that combine good design, good function, and good quality with low prices and that create a better everyday life for the majority of people.
5. IKEA inspects the supplier's operations to ensure there is an awareness of child labor issues.
6. So they could see for themselves the conditions under which their goods were produced.

Words and Phrases from the Reading (page 109)

1. g 2. f 3. a 4. i 5. d
6. h 7. j 8. c 9. e 10. b

1. a 2. b 3. a

UNIT 11

Listening (page 115)

1. A whole body scan.
2. The patient pays.
3. There is no pain but the patient is exposed to a lot of radiation.
4. From hundreds of dollars to over $1,000.
5. The scan could uncover a disease that he might have, such as an early form of cancer. Then he could be treated before he became sick.

6. The patient is exposed to a lot of radiation.
7. The scans reveal minor conditions.
8. When the scan shows something that is not there, it is a "false positive."
9. A patient might undergo tests or get treatment he doesn't need if there is a "false positive."
10. A thorough yearly exam.

Words and Phrases About Medicine (page 116)

1. symptoms 2. condition 3. procedure
4. prescription 5. diagnosed 6. specialist

1. d 2. b 3. a 4. c

(page 117)

1. under the weather 2. a touch of something
3. symptoms 4. prescription 5. condition
6. diagnosed 7. procedure 8. prone to
9. side effects 10. specialist

From the News (page 121)

1. a 2. b 3. a 4. b 5. b 6. a 7. b

Words and Phrases from the Reading (page 122)

1. d 2. f 3. j 4. b 5. i
6. a 7. c 8. g 9. h 10. e

(page 123)

1. a 2. a 3. a 4. b 5. a 6. b 7. a

UNIT 12

Listening (page 128)

Reporter's facts:
> 1400 years ago.
> In 1300.
> 100,000–200,000 inhabitants.
> 1987.
> Wal-Mart built a store.

Protester's main points:
> Wal-Mart is stealing their cultural heritage.
> The store is huge.
> Wal-Mart has over 600 other stores in Mexico.
> They built on an archaeological site.
> Wants to preserve the collective past and cultural identity.
> Store will damage spirit of the place.
> Wants to be able to conduct archaeological digs in the future.

Employee's main points:
> The unemployment rate in Mexico is high.
> The store brings 200 new jobs.
> The salaries are better than at other companies.
> You have to make sacrifices to support your family.

Shopper's main points:
> Local stores have high prices.
> Wal-Mart has convenient location.
> Many local people happy that store was built.
> Important to keep up with the times.
> Can't live in the past.

WORDS AND PHRASES ABOUT CULTURAL HERITAGE (PAGE 129)

1. gerontology 2. location 3. segregation
4. native 5. low-income housing

(page 130)

1. b 2. d 3. a 4. c

1. living in the past 2. Assimilation
3. break with tradition 4. archaeology
5. a time-honored custom 6. gentrification
7. expatriate 8. artifacts
9. the sprit of ancient Greece

From the News (page 134)

1. A traditional, working class neighborhood.
2. Residents include young professionals, students, and American expatriates. There are cocktail bars instead of butchers and fashion boutiques instead of bakeries. The vendors in the open-air markets can't make enough money. The neighborhoods are becoming too expensive.
3. People think of social dislocation.
4. There are more supermarkets, cocktail bars, pizzerias, cafes, and stylish shops.
5. Many European professionals are moving there. Romans are leaving.
6. New residents shop after working hours at supermarkets; older residents shopped in the open-air markets.
7. The government is pursuing a master plan to preserve the character of the neighborhoods.
8. That their new neighbors get used to shopping outdoors.

Words and Phrases from the Reading (page 135)

Down	*Across*
1. refurbishing	3. boast
2. residents	8. quaintness
4. open-air	10. connotation
5. patronize	
6. tightknit	
7. ironic	
9. succumbed	

(page 136)

1. b 2. a 3. b 4. b

1. run in the family 2. run errands 3. run across
4. run out of 5. run up 6. run up against
7. run through 8. run after

AUDIOSCRIPT

UNIT 1

(page 3) Listening

Woman: Good morning.

Man: Good morning. What are you reading in the paper?

Woman: I'm reading the science section. There's an intriguing article on MRIs. The new uses of this technology are pretty amazing, even a bit alarming.

Man: MRI—doesn't that stand for magnetic resonance imaging?

Woman: Yes.

Man: Aren't MRIs just used to locate medical problems, such as a torn tendon or arthritis in a joint?

Woman: Yes, they're used to scan the body and look for medical problems. They basically show a picture of the inside of the body.

Man: MRIs have been around for some time. What's so amazing about them?

Woman: Well, in the past, scientists have used them to locate possible brain damage, among other things. But now, according to this article, scientists are using more advanced types of MRIs to analyze activity in specific regions of the brain.

Man: That sounds interesting. Tell me more.

Woman: The article says that scientists can study these pictures of the brain and figure out what you're feeling based on which area of the brain "lights up."

Man: That's amazing! You mean these scientists can eavesdrop on what you're feeling? How exactly does it work?

Woman: These MRIs reveal changes in oxygen use, which indicates increased or decreased activity in certain areas of the brain. And since the scientists know which regions of the brain are associated with specific emotions . . .

Man: . . . they might actually be able to identify what a person is feeling?

Woman: Exactly. Doesn't it sound like an invasion of privacy?

Man: Perhaps, but it is fascinating, and the technology must have some positive uses.

Woman: Well, the article mentioned how the government could use the MRI to test criminals before releasing them from prison to see if they are still violent.

Man: Well, that sounds like a positive use. But by law, don't prison inmates have a right to privacy, too? I mean, wouldn't they have to give their consent?

Woman: I suppose. The article also says that employers could use the MRI to test job applicants to see if they are honest or whether they suffer from emotional problems like depression.

Man: Hmmm. I'm not sure I like the sound of that. I wouldn't want my bosses to have access to my inner feelings or emotional states. That's really none of their business.

Woman: I agree. Another example here is about advertisers possibly using this technology to help with their marketing strategies. They could use brain scans to see how customers respond to advertising. Then they would change their advertising schemes in order to sell more products.

Man: Well, that's a scary thought. We don't want advertisers reading our minds, do we?

Woman: Certainly not. Luckily, the equipment is really expensive, so not many people can use it, at least not yet.

Man: Well, I'm glad to hear that, but who knows how this sort of technology will be used in the future?

UNIT 2

(page 16) Listening

Man: Hi, Sarah. That was an awesome race. You really outdid yourself today, don't you think?

Woman: You think so? I guess, I did do pretty well, but I could've done even better.

Man: Hey—you just moved up a notch and now you're eligible to go to the championships next week. That's something to be very proud of.

Woman: I suppose so, but lately I have been feeling as if I'll never be fast enough.

	My times are only a bit better than they were six months ago.
Man:	What do you mean, Sarah? Think of how far you've come in the past six months. Remember when you first started running? Your times were much slower and you just didn't have the stamina you have now. Look at you today! You're strong! You have made incredible progress.
Woman:	Well, I am doing better than I was six months or a year ago, but I still need to be a lot faster to win. What about all the other runners who are so much faster than I am? How can I compete with them?
Man:	Sarah, each athlete progresses at a different pace. You've got to be patient. You are doing the best you can right now, and you've shown enormous dedication to your sport.
Woman:	I probably shouldn't tell you this, but. . . . A friend of mine told me about something I could take to build my muscles and improve my speed.
Man:	Something you could take? Do you mean a drug to help you get stronger and faster? Don't even think about it! You and I have worked so hard during training to build up your strength and speed. There is no shortcut to becoming strong and fast . . . it takes hard work and training.
Woman:	Well, my friend took the drug and she said it really helped her run faster. Plus she said she had fewer aches and pains so she could work out longer and race harder.
Man:	Sarah, using drugs is an artificial way to mask the pain of training. Being an athlete is hard work—no pain, no gain! If you cover the pain by taking a drug, you could hurt yourself because you won't know when to stop before you cause an injury.
Woman:	Well, I still think about trying it, if it would mean faster times and more medals. Right now, nothing seems more important to me than being the fastest.
Man:	Did your friend tell you that those drugs have severe health effects too? They can hurt your heart or cause other serious damage. Some people even died from taking those drugs.

Woman:	Really? No, my friend didn't mention that.
Man:	Are you willing to sacrifice your health for medals? Life is lived in the long run, you know. Don't you want to live a long, healthy life?
Woman:	Of course I do, but still it's not fair. I know other runners who are taking the drugs. How can I compete with them?
Man:	Just because someone else is doing it doesn't mean that you have to as well. I wish you would just concentrate on your gifts. You're a good enough athlete to win on your own without the help of performance-enhancing drugs. That is something to be proud of. I want you to win those medals fair and square because you are truly the fastest.
Woman:	Well, you may be right, but I'm so eager to win, not some time off in the future, but now.

Unit 3

(page 29) Listening

Woman:	I have been using this new peer-to-peer network to download some great music. Do you want me to copy some songs for you? I can burn you a CD.
Man:	No, thanks. I use an online store to purchase my favorite songs. It's easy and it's only 99 cents a song.
Woman:	But why pay anything when there is so much music available out there— for free?
Man:	Well, for one thing, copying music from those free sites is illegal, and I don't feel like getting sued by the recording industry.
Woman:	I doubt that anyone would ever know. I mean, how could anybody catch you? There are just too many people sharing music files over the Internet on peer-to-peer networks. The recording industry can't prosecute all of us. Besides, people make their own copies of music all the time to give to friends. Sharing music over the Internet isn't any different.
Man:	Well, copying CDs is illegal, too. But downloading from free music sites really took off and that's when recording companies started suing people.

Basically, music and song lyrics are protected by copyright laws, and if you reproduce them without paying, you are violating the rights of the artists and the companies.

Woman: I guess I understand the law, but don't you think that music is overpriced?

Man: Maybe, but did you ever think about how expensive it is to produce music? Think of all the people involved: the songwriter, the singer, the musicians, the producer, the recording engineer, the cover artist, and the marketing and advertising people. They all need to make a living, just like anyone else.

Woman: What about the many new musicians and bands who don't have a recording company behind them? These peer-to-peer networks give new musicians access to a wider audience. Independent and emerging artists want publicity, which the Internet provides.

Man: I think it's fine if artists *choose* to offer their music for free just to get noticed, but it should be their choice. If you download uncopyrighted music, you're *not* breaking the law, but if you or your children are downloading copyrighted music, you *are* breaking the law.

Woman: Can parents actually get in trouble if their kids download and share songs without paying?

Man: They sure can.

Woman: Well, I don't think that's fair.

Man: Well, recording companies are trying to make everyone aware of the law, and hold people responsible. Universities are now starting to block students' Internet access because they don't want to be liable for illegal downloads.

Woman: Well, I don't agree with that either. Why should the university be responsible? If you ask me, the music industry is making a lot of money and has too much control over how people get music.

Man: Maybe, but until it changes, be careful!

UNIT 4

(page 39) Listening

Employee: Oh . . . I just can't stand it anymore.

Friend: What's the matter?

Employee: Well, you know I work in the factory here in town.

Friend: Yes.

Employee: And for some time now, the company hasn't been disposing of chemical waste properly. I started to notice this about six months ago. The disposal system broke down. But no one came to fix it.

Friend: So how did the company get rid of the chemicals?

Employee: Well, from what I could see, they were just dumping them in the river that runs along the factory.

Friend: The river that runs through town? People swim and fish in that river. If the company is polluting the river with dangerous chemicals, people should know about it. Did you say anything?

Employee: I spoke to my supervisor, but he told me not to worry about it. He said it was all under control.

Friend: So, was it under control?

Employee: No. It kept happening. So I told my supervisor again. He told me to keep my mouth shut and mind my own business. I tried to ask some of the other guys what they thought about it, but no one wants to say anything. I also tried to talk to one of the upper managers about the problem, but she didn't answer my phone calls.

Friend: What are you going to do?

Employee: I don't know. What the company is doing is wrong and apparently people at the top know about it.

Friend: Well, you could blow the whistle.

Employee: What do you mean?

Friend: If the company is doing something illegal and is not attempting to fix it, you could tell the authorities.

Employee: But I'd just feel like an informer! Plus, I don't have any idea how I would go about doing that. Who do I tell? What would happen to me? What if the factory closes? My buddies work there. How would they make a living?

Friend: You do have a lot to consider before blowing the whistle. You have to be willing to take the consequences.

Employee: Well, if I were willing, how would I go about it?

Friend: Well, first you have to try to talk to management about the problem.

Employee:	I've already done that, but they won't listen.
Friend:	The next step is to ask yourself if the wrongdoing is bad enough for you— or anyone—to speak out.
Employee:	This is fairly bad. Don't you think?
Friend:	Yes. Then ask yourself if you are willing to risk what might happen to you.
Employee:	You mean retaliation on the part of the company?
Friend:	Right. What happens if you lose your job? Or are demoted to a lesser-paying job, a bad shift, or a job that makes your life difficult? Are you willing to stand for that?
Employee:	I'm not sure. I really need my job to pay the bills.
Friend:	And even if you don't get the axe or a demotion, you might experience intimidation at work. Can you handle that?
Employee:	I like to think I can.
Friend:	Also, consider how this could affect your family. What do they feel about the situation? Are they willing to stand by you no matter what?
Employee:	Well, I'm not sure. We need to have a heart-to-heart talk. I know this could have a bad effect on them financially and emotionally. Still I think they will stand by me.
Friend:	If you decide to blow the whistle, you'll have to hire a lawyer in order to decide whether to proceed with the case.
Employee:	Blowing the whistle is a lot of work.
Friend:	It is a *lot* of work. Like I said, you have to be ready for the battle.
Employee:	If my family backs me up, and I think they will, I'm ready.

UNIT 5

(page 50) Listening

Rick:	Hi. Rick Randolph here for another week of "What Do You Have to Say?" On this week's show, I'm going to ask people what they think about reality TV. By now, all of you out there must have seen one of the many reality TV shows. The goal of many of these shows is to win, which means someone else has to lose.

While winning itself is not necessarily bad, often the contestants will do anything possible to win—lie, cheat, or gang up on one person. The losers are often humiliated. And millions of people are watching.

What I want to know is—What's the fascination with reality TV? Should we be watching these shows and encouraging producers to make more and more of them? What do you have to say? Here's our first person. Excuse me, miss. Do you have a second?

Woman 1:	Hey! Don't I know you? It's Rick . . . Rick . . .
Rick:	Yeah, Rick Randolph here on TV. I have a question for you. Have you seen the popular show called "Big Brother"? It's shown all over the United States and Europe.
Woman 1:	Yeah. I used to live in London, and the show was really popular there. On the show, a group of people were living in a house with cameras in every room. Every week, they voted someone out of the house. And the public could call in and vote too. The last person remaining in the house won a lot of money.
Rick:	What do you think about shows like that? Are they entertaining?
Woman 1:	Personally, I don't like them. "Big Brother" reminded me of team sports in high school—you know, that awful feeling of not being picked until the end. I get that same feeling when I watch reality TV shows. They're all about public humiliation and rejection. They're not very compassionate, and that's not a good thing.
Rick:	Thanks for sharing your thoughts. Let's see if we can get another opinion. Here's someone. Ah, sir, can I ask you a question?
Man 1:	Who, me? . . . um . . . well, OK. What?
Rick:	I'd like to hear your opinions of reality TV. Have you heard of the TV show in Germany called "Big Diet," where overweight people try to lose weight week after week? If they don't lose the right amount every week, they have to leave the show.
Man 1:	You're kidding me. That's a TV show?
Rick:	Yes. What do you think about that type of program?

Man 1:	Well, I don't watch much reality TV, and I definitely wouldn't watch that type of show. What really bothers me is that the producers are making money on this type of entertainment. Why should anyone profit from another person's embarrassment or failure? What's the value?
Rick:	Well, you know, people on the show have lost a lot of weight. Doesn't that count for something? I mean, the show does have some positive effect.
Man 1:	Well, I suppose you could look at it that way. If a show like "Big Diet" motivates someone to improve, perhaps it's OK.
Rick:	How about "The Apprentice"? Have you heard about that show?
Man 1:	"The Apprentice"? You mean the one with that rich businessman, Donald Trump? The people on the show have to solve business problems, right?
Rick:	Right. The winner of "The Apprentice" gets a great, high-paying job working with Trump. Pretty great prize, don't you think?
Man 1:	Well, I don't think I'd like to work with Trump myself, but my friend works in the business world and he finds the show very educational. He says the people have to really work together and solve problems. Yeah, that show is worth watching.
Rick:	Well, thanks for your time. Let's see. Here's a woman who looks like she could be a fan. Ma'am, do you have a second to voice your opinions about reality TV?
Woman 2:	Sure! What do you want to know? I've always wanted to be on TV. Hi, everyone out there!
Rick:	I'm interviewing people about reality TV. Have you seen a show called "American Idol," the one where young people get up on stage to show off their talents?
Woman 2:	You bet I have. I *love* that show. All those brave people get up and sing.
Rick:	How do you feel about the losers? Sometimes the judges are pretty mean to them.
Woman 2:	Oh, but the winners feel so good! They have a chance they might never have gotten otherwise—a once-in-a-lifetime opportunity. I feel so happy

	for them! Plus, the ones the judges don't like—the losers—someone needs to tell them they aren't talented. They need to know they just don't have what it takes.
Rick:	Well, I suppose. Thank you for your time. Let's talk to one more person. Sir, can I ask you a question?
Man 2:	Shoot. What's up?
Rick:	I'm taking an informal poll here. I want to understand why people watch reality TV and whether we should encourage that kind of programming. What do you think? What do people see in reality TV?
Man 2:	I think people like these shows because they are similar to the struggles we face in our own lives.
Rick:	So that's why reality TV appeals to you? Can you give me an example?
Man 2:	Well, take a show like "Survivor," for instance. I like watching the people figure out what to do when they don't have any modern tools. Only the strongest or smartest ones survive.
Rick:	So you enjoy watching the skill involved?
Man 2:	Yeah, I do. I like the problem solving and the suspense. I'm trying to figure out what will happen next. Now that's entertainment!
Rick:	There you have it, folks. People just don't agree about the appeal of reality TV. Some like these shows because they're exciting and they reveal people's strengths and talents. Others think the shows are a waste of time because they're all about humiliating people in public and profiting from others' misfortunes. Let me know which side you're on. If you have an opinion you'd like to share about reality TV, send me an e-mail. I'll read your responses next week when I'm back for another "What Do You Have to Say." Until then, I'm Rick Randolph wishing you good night.

UNIT 6

(page 59) Listening

Student:	Hi, Mr. Mason. Thanks for agreeing to meet with me on such short notice.
Counselor:	Sure, anytime, Jason. How is your job search going? With all of your

	qualifications, I'm sure you've had a lot of offers.
Student:	Well, after taking your class last semester, I learned a lot about finding a good job. I've been sending out lots of résumés, applying for jobs, and I've gone on four interviews so far.
Counselor:	That sounds like good news.
Student:	Yeah, I thought so, at first. Some companies seemed really interested in meeting me when I talked to them on the phone about my computer background. But after the interviews, not a single one called me back.
Counselor:	Well, how did you handle the interviews? Did you get nervous or tongue-tied?
Student:	No, the interviews were no problem. I did really well. I was never at a loss for words. I'd done my research on each company so I'd be prepared. That's what confuses me.
Counselor:	Let me ask you this. What did you wear to the interviews?
Student:	What do you mean? I wore something like what I'm wearing now— jeans, boots. You know me: I'm not a suit and tie kind of guy. What are you getting at?
Counselor:	Well, I hate to say this, but the problem may have nothing to do with your qualifications. It may be how you look. These employers may be afraid to hire you because you look too casual, too trendy, too hip. You just don't look the part of a corporate computer programmer.
Student:	Really? You think that these companies won't hire me because I wear what I like and I have purple hair and piercings? Do you think that's right?
Counselor:	Don't get me wrong. I don't object to your outfits and hairstyle, but some employers will.
Student:	Well, I think that's unfair. It's a form of discrimination in a way.
Counselor:	That may be true, but the way you dress may be narrowing your job opportunities.
Student:	You really think that these places rejected me just because I didn't wear appropriate business attire? I mean this is the twenty-first century—the Information Age. Hasn't all that changed?
Counselor:	Yes, in some places it has, but in others not so much. I agree that appearance shouldn't matter in many jobs, but the fact is that it does. Some businesses want to project a certain image. And that image may not coincide with your particular style.
Student:	That seems pretty narrow-minded to me. I just can't see myself changing how I look. That's like trying to change who I am.
Counselor:	Well, I just want you to think it over. As you continue your job search, consider what I've said. Decide which is more important to you—the job or how you look.
Student:	That's a tough one. I'll think it over. But right now, I might just be happier working for a company that cared more about me doing the job well than my appearance.

UNIT 7

(page 70) Listening

Gretchen:	Hey, Mick. Is that you? I haven't seen you in ages.
Mick:	Gretchen. It's great running into you. I've missed the old gang so much since we moved. I hardly ever get back to the neighborhood. How are things with you?
Gretchen:	Things are good. I'm going to school at night and working in the day. Speaking of the neighborhood, do you remember the older lady who lived down the street from you—the one in the rundown yellow house?
Mick:	Sure do. Virginia Stone. I remember her well. I used to shovel snow for her when I was in junior high. How's she doing?
Gretchen:	She's fine, but you aren't going to believe this. It turns out she's really really rich—a multimillionaire, actually.
Mick:	Are you for real?
Gretchen:	It's a fact, but nobody would have guessed it from the way she's been living. I guess she wanted it that way—to keep quiet about her money. But a local reporter found out that she'd been donating a lot of money. So he interviewed her and wrote her up in the local paper.

Mick:	So what did she say? Is she going to buy an exotic island or build a mansion of some kind? Or just fix up that house?
Gretchen:	No, not at all. Believe it or not she has been giving a lot of money away. For the past few years, she has made huge donations to various arts organizations across the country.
Mick:	Wow, she's not your typical millionaire. Why is she giving away so much money?
Gretchen:	Evidently, she always wanted to be a painter but decided she wasn't good enough herself. Now she wants to help young artists who are just starting out. She's been donating millions of dollars to various states to fund arts programs and grants for artists. She has helped to build artist studios and daycare centers for artists with kids.
Mick:	That's cool! Imagine if more millionaires and billionaires were like that. The world would be different. Don't you think?
Gretchen:	Yeah, so many superrich people seem to hold on to their money. They hoard it so that they can live in walled estates, have chauffeurs and private limousines, and lead lives of unbelievable luxury. When you consider how much need there is in the world, they seem pretty greedy to me.
Mick:	Now you're being too simplistic. Just because people are rich doesn't mean they're greedy. Think about it. If I became a millionaire overnight, I'd definitely want to spend my money on all kinds of things for myself. I'd buy designer clothes and a sports car. I'd build my dream house. I'd travel around the world. Be honest, wouldn't you do the same?
Gretchen:	I don't know. Maybe at first I would buy certain things. But then I think I'd feel guilty about keeping all my money for myself. Objects just aren't that important to me. I'd want to share my money somehow and try to do good works with it.
Mick:	So you'd be like Virginia or those rock stars who donate money and work hard for humanitarian causes? Like Bono from U2. He's committed time and money to a lot of good causes

	like helping African nations manage their debt so they can improve health care and education.
Gretchen:	Yes, or someone like the actress Angelina Jolie.
Mick:	The actress in *Alexander* and *Girl Interrupted*?
Gretchen:	I was so impressed when she became the Goodwill Ambassador for the United Nations on behalf of refugees.
Mick:	She did that?
Gretchen:	Yes. She was so concerned about equality and the protection of human rights that she went around the world visiting refugee camps in places like Ecuador, Tanzania, Kenya, Cambodia, Thailand, and Pakistan.
Mick:	I think it's great when people with lots of money choose to help others. But I don't think you can expect it. Do you really believe that people with millions or even billions of dollars have a moral responsibility to help others?
Gretchen:	Yes, I do. . . . Don't look at me like that. I know what you're thinking. You think I'm being too idealistic.
Mick:	Perhaps.
Gretchen:	Well, I may be idealistic, but I do think that the superrich should do something to help people who don't even have the basic necessities.

Unit 8

(page 82) Listening

Woman:	So, you've just graduated from college. What are your plans?
Man:	I've decided to stay here for now. I want to be near my family.
Woman:	I'm surprised to hear that. Don't you want to move to the big city? This town is pretty small. Not much is happening here, and there certainly aren't any exciting job opportunities.
Man:	I know this town has problems and it is pretty small, but I want to help make it grow. As for a job, I plan to help out with the family business. My father would like me to take over the business one day.
Woman:	Well, I am moving to the city. I already have a great job offer. I'm really looking forward to starting my career. I have lots of plans.

Man: You always did like the city and city life. I'm sure you'll be happy living there. But I could never move away for long. This is my home and my whole family is here.

Woman: That's interesting. I love my family but I haven't lived close to them for years, not since I started college.

Man: Don't you miss them?

Woman: Of course I do. But we keep in touch by phone and e-mail, and I go home as often as I can. I always make it a point to see them on holidays and other special occasions. Of course, they wish I lived closer, but they want me to live my own life.

Man: My entire family lives here and we're all very close. We see each other as often as we can—sometimes daily. I think I'd be pretty lonely without that type of connection. Plus, my parents helped me pay for college. They have worked hard to build their business. It's time for me to give something back.

Woman: I understand what you're saying, but what about your own dreams? Didn't you have another career in mind when you were in college? You worked hard to get your degree. Wouldn't you like to use it?

Man: Sure, I had lots of dreams, but I'm going to realize them here. I'll try to apply what I learned in school to expanding and improving the family business. And on the side, I'd also like to start an amateur theater group.

Woman: But you could do so much more. There are so many opportunities out there. Why limit yourself?

Man: Well, I guess I don't look at it that way. I don't feel limited here. I feel good about helping my family and I'm planning to make an impact on town life.

Woman: I hope you're right, but I'm afraid that staying here will be a dead end for you. What will your life be like in ten years?

Man: Neither of us can predict where we'll be ten years from now, but I am fond of this area and I don't want to see it die out. I'm sad that so many people my age have decided to move away.

Woman: Won't you feel trapped by all your obligations to your family?

Man: No. To me, family comes first. That's just the way I was raised. I'm especially fond of my older sister. She's a single parent with two kids. I enjoy babysitting for her and watching my niece and nephew grow.

Woman: You really are a homebody, aren't you?

Man: I guess so. I'm a real family person.

Woman: Well, let's promise to write to each other. I want to keep in touch.

Man: Sure thing. Good luck!

Woman: Yeah, you too.

UNIT 9

(page 93) Listening

Father: Hi, honey. Look at this new computer I just bought. It's the very latest model.

Mother: A new computer? Sweetie, we don't need a new computer. We have one that works just fine.

Father: I know ours is not that old, but you know technology changes so fast.

I want our kids to have the very best technology. It will make their lives so much easier. They spend so much time online, surfing the net. They should have a state-of-the-art computer.

Mother: I know you only want what's best for our kids, but I have been thinking lately about how much time our kids spend on the computer, on their cell phones, and watching DVDs.

Father: Well, that's what most of their friends do.

Mother: Yes, but don't you remember when we were kids? After school we would play outside, visit our friends, do more social things. Sometimes we'd just spend some quiet time reading a book. Nowadays, kids are spending so much time indoors with all these electronic devices. What about being with other people? I worry about the lack of social interaction.

Father: Well, when our kids are online, they might be in a chat room and actually interacting with people who live in an entirely different part of the world.

We never had that type of opportunity growing up, short of getting on a plane and flying somewhere, or calling someone we might know. Our kids are interacting, but in a different way.

Mother: Well, even when it comes to chat rooms I have some concerns. Have you seen how the kids write to each other? They don't use full sentences, they use all kinds of symbols and shorthand to represent emotions. How good is that for their writing skills?

Father: I don't worry about our kids' writing abilities. Chat rooms are just conversations.

Mother: Don't you worry about who our kids might meet out there in—what do you call it?—cyberspace?

Father: Really, dear. I think it is a great opportunity. You know, times change. We have to keep up or we'll be left behind. Our kids are going to be living in a much more technologically advanced time than the one we grew up in. They have to keep up in order to be competitive in the job market. It's their future that's at stake here.

Mother: You may be right, but I am not sure I like the direction our society is taking. Sometimes, I think there's too much technology and information available. I often wish we could go back to a simpler time.

Father: Well, there's no way to turn back the clocks. And we want our kids to be able to flourish.

Mother: Yes, of course. I guess, I just feel as if we speak a different language than our kids. I mean they're talking about things I have never heard of. I sometimes feel we have nothing in common anymore. I don't know how to use all these new devices and technologies.

Father: Well, use the opportunity to ask. Let your kids teach you something.

Mother: Just the other day I noticed they were listening to a new CD. Some music I had never heard of. I wanted to be part of what they were doing. The song stopped and I asked if they wanted me to turn the CD over. They just burst out laughing!

Father: Oh, sweetie. I am sure they were laughing with you, not at you! You don't have to turn a CD over!

Mother: Well, now I know. See how behind the times I am!

Father/Mother: (both laugh)

Unit 10

(page 104) Listening

Receptionist: Good afternoon, Allied Industries. How can I help you?

Yolanda: Hello, I am trying to reach Melinda Basso, please.

Receptionist: May I ask who is calling?

Yolanda: Yes, this is Yolanda Ramos. Ms. Basso agreed to do a phone interview with me at 2:30.

Receptionist: One moment. I'll transfer you.

Melinda: Hello. This is Melinda.

Yolanda: Hi, this is Yolanda Ramos. We spoke earlier. You agreed to let me interview you about Allied Industries this afternoon. Is this still a good time?

Melinda: Yes, certainly. Hi, Yolanda. How are you today?

Yolanda: I'm fine, thanks. Ever since I moved to Omaha this year, I've been hearing good things about your company. And I wanted to find out more.

Melinda: Yes, Allied is a great place to work. What would you like to know about the company?

Yolanda: Well, my background is in marketing. I'm interested in working as a marketing assistant. I have several years' experience, and I wondered what the salary range would be for that sort of position.

Melinda: I can't quote you an exact figure, but the salary range for marketing assistants is probably somewhere between twenty-five and thirty thousand dollars, depending on your qualifications.

Yolanda: Really? That's a little low. I made quite a bit more than that at my previous job in Los Angeles. You see, I am paying off student loans, and I have a family to support.

Melinda: Well, we think that the salary is competitive for this part of the country, and we offer many other benefits besides salary that are worth a lot.

Yolanda:	I know that health care is very expensive. What kinds of health care coverage do you offer?
Melinda:	Allied employees have a variety of health plans to choose from, including HMOs and Point of Service plans for people who want to choose their own doctors.
Yolanda:	What about professional development? Do you have any on-the-job training?
Melinda:	Yes, we offer online courses and on-site workshops about areas of the business, and we also reimburse employees for any job-related education.
Yolanda:	That would be great for me. I've been taking classes toward my master's degree at night. And what about work hours? Is there any possibility of working flexible hours?
Melinda:	Employees have the option of working 8 to 4, 9 to 5, or 10 to 6. Sometimes, during a busy season, we do expect employees to put in some extra hours.
Yolanda:	Overtime would be hard for me right now. I'm taking classes at night and my two-year-old daughter is in daycare. My husband and I take turns picking her up.
Melinda:	Well, our CEO is a working mother herself. And she insisted that Allied set up a small daycare facility for employees whose children are under five.
Yolanda:	That's a great company benefit! And what about vacation and personal days?
Melinda:	During your first year, you would have five vacation days, three personal days, and five sick days.
Yolanda:	That's *not* a lot of time for vacation.
Melinda:	Well, in your second year, you would get an additional five vacation days.
Yolanda:	I guess I was spoiled at my previous job. We had four weeks off the first year. One final question: I heard that Allied was donating money to the local elementary school to purchase new books and computers. Is that true?
Melinda:	Yes, our CEO believes that educating children is one of society's most important obligations. Each year, the company donates a percentage of its

profits to an educational institution in our community. This year, we're giving to the elementary school. Next year, it will be the high school.

Yolanda:	Well, your CEO sounds like an ethical person, and Allied does sound like a good place to work. The only drawbacks for me are the lower pay and the lack of time off to spend with my family.
Melinda:	Well, think it over. Call me if you are seriously considering a job with us, and I'll help you set up an interview with Human Resources.
Yolanda:	Thanks so much. I really appreciate your taking the time to talk to me. I've learned a lot about Allied.
Melinda:	You're welcome. Good luck on your job search.
Yolanda:	Thanks. Goodbye.

UNIT 11

(page 115) Listening

Dr. Alvarez:	Mr. Lansing, nice to see you again. How are you? Come in, please.
Mr. Lansing:	Hi, Dr. Alvarez. Thanks for seeing me today.
Dr. Alvarez:	Sure, no problem. What can I do for you?
Mr. Lansing:	Well, as I am sure you have heard, there is a new procedure called a whole body scan, where a CT scan is done of the whole body.
Dr. Alvarez:	Yes, I am familiar with this kind of scan.
Mr. Lansing:	It sounds like a test I might want to take. I wanted to get your opinion about it.
Dr. Alvarez:	Well, from the outset, I want you to know that your insurance company won't pay for the procedure.
Mr. Lansing:	Yes, I know that. If I decide to have the scan, I know I will have to pay.
Dr. Alvarez:	It can cost a lot; from hundreds of dollars to over a thousand dollars.
Mr. Lansing:	Right. That's what I was told. I might be willing to spend that much, but first I want to find out what you think about this kind of scan.
Dr. Alvarez:	Well, it's a full body scan—like a three-dimensional x-ray of your

whole body. Most people choose to have such a scan *not* because they are sick, but because they want to know if they *might* become sick in the future. They are afraid that they might have some hidden illness that has not become a problem yet.

Mr. Lansing: And I've been told that there is no pain. Is that right?

Dr. Alvarez: There is no pain involved, but the patient is exposed to a lot of radiation during the scan, much more than patients are during a traditional x-ray, and that could be unhealthy for you. I suggest you look into that aspect of the scans more carefully.

Mr. Lansing: I will. What interests me most is that I could uncover a disease I might have, such as an early form of cancer that has not made me sick yet. Then I could have it treated before I became sick. That could save my life!

Dr. Alvarez: In a few rare instances, a full body scan detects a cancer before it has become a problem, but most of the time these scans only reveal very minor conditions that are not life-threatening or even dangerous.

Mr. Lansing: Really?

Dr. Alvarez: Yes. In fact, sometimes the scans lead to unnecessary surgical procedures. I read about one case in which a patient had a full body scan and discovered that there was some sort of growth on his lung. The patient had a surgical lung biopsy and, as it turned out, his condition was not dangerous. However, the patient suffered complications from the surgery; you know surgery always carries certain risks. He ended up spending a week in the hospital, and he had to take time off from work to recuperate from the surgery. So in the end, the scan created more problems than it solved, and it also cost him a lot of money in medical bills.

Mr. Lansing: I wouldn't want to go through something like that.

Dr. Alvarez: So one question you have to ask is, what are you going to do if the scan detects something in your body that *might* be dangerous?

Mr. Lansing: I'm not sure, but that's an important consideration.

Dr. Alvarez: Also, you have to consider the possibility that the scan will show something that is *not* there at all. This sort of result is called a "false positive." You might have to pay for additional tests or seek treatment for something that isn't there. So the full body scan is an expensive procedure to undergo in order to turn up something that *might,* just *might,* be important.

Mr. Lansing: You really have to weigh the benefits against the drawbacks of these scans, don't you?

Dr. Alvarez: Yes. You have to weigh your strong need to know whether you are healthy against the drawbacks and risks of the scan. There's the high amount of radiation, the high cost of the procedure, and as I mentioned, the false positives and the potential for unnecessary tests and surgery. I recommend a thorough yearly physical to everyone. You will get a good assessment of your health, and the risks are very low.

Mr. Lansing: OK, well, thanks for sharing this information with me.

Dr. Alvarez: No problem, any time. Take care of yourself.

Mr. Lansing: Thanks, I will. Have a nice day.

UNIT 12

(page 128) Listening

Reporter: Good evening. I'm standing in front of the ruins of Teotihuacán—an ancient city that flourished in central Mexico approximately 1,400 years ago. The site became the subject of controversy a few months back when Wal-Mart, the world's largest retail chain, began quietly constructing a 71,000-square-foot store here. When the Aztecs came to this place in 1300 and saw these magnificent temples and pyramids, they believed the site was sacred. To many contemporary Mexicans, the area represents an important cultural legacy. At its peak, Teotihuacán controlled an intricate network of commercial routes that stretched in every direction. The inhabitants traded with people as far away as in Guatemala and northern Mexico.

Once Teotihuacán was a thriving city of 100,000 to 200,000 inhabitants. Now all that remains is the main ceremonial center where the ancient pyramids and temples are located. The United Nations designated Teotihuacán a World Heritage Site in 1987 in an effort to preserve this Mexican treasure. Nevertheless, this archaeological site is in danger because of increased settlement close to the pyramids and the recent construction of this superstore. Today when Wal-Mart opened its store near Teotihuacán, more than 200 people lined up to shop. But while some people are looking for a bargain, others are protesting the presence of a store so close to the archaeological site. Let's interview some people and see what they have to say on the subject. Sir, I see you are protesting the opening of this store. What are your concerns?

Protester: I'm very upset about the store because it was built only a few steps away from the ruins of a great civilization. Wal-Mart is stealing our cultural heritage. The pyramids of the Sun and the Moon, the temples, all the remains of Teotihuacán evoke the spirit of ancient times. We should be preserving this place, not shopping here.

Reporter: But Wal-Mart claims that it has built the store in an approved area. Weren't there other small businesses here before Wal-Mart came along?

Protester: Yes, other businesses existed here before, but they were small, locally owned stores. Such stores blend in. This store is huge and imposing. It just doesn't belong near this sacred site. Wal-Mart already has over 600 stores in Mexico. The company is making billions of dollars here. Why did it need to build this particular store on sacred ground?

Reporter: Some people say that no damage has been done to the site during the construction of the store. They also believe that few, if any, artifacts remain to be discovered in this region.

Protester: That's not true. During the construction of the parking lot, an artifact was found. This is a culturally rich area. Surely, other artifacts are waiting to be found. Now that the store has gone up, we will never be able to conduct archaeological digs again.

Reporter: Well, thank you for sharing your opinions with us. Now, let's step inside the store and talk to one of the employees. Hello, ma'am. I want to know how you feel about the new Wal-Mart. What do you think of these protesters outside? I am sure you're glad to have a job, but what about cultural preservation? Aren't the ruins here important to you?

Worker: I know a lot of people think that this site should be preserved. I understand that, but I have been unemployed for months. The unemployment rate in Mexico is very high. This store brings with it almost 200 new jobs. And the salaries here are better than anything at a nearby company. I love the ruins here, and so do my parents. Of course, it's sad to see the area change, but sometimes you have to make sacrifices to support yourself and your family.

Reporter: Thank you for sharing your perspective. Let's see what this shopper has to say about the new store. Sir, you are stocking up on lots of items. How do you feel about this new store and its location?

Shopper: I'm very happy to have the store here and I like its location. You know, I used to have to drive more than 15 miles to buy these items at low prices. All my local stores have such high prices. Shopping here is going to save me both time and money. Having the store so close to home will be a great convenience to me.

Reporter: Wal-Mart claims that it wants people all over Mexico to have access to a wide variety of products at affordable prices. The company says it is not fair that people living in small towns have to pay higher prices and have less choice. Do you think the store represents progress for the local community?

Shopper: Yes, I do. Many locals were happy that the store was built.

Reporter: And does it bother you that the store is located so close to an important historical site? Some people feel the

Shopper: site is sacred and should be protected.

Shopper: Well, the temples and pyramids are still here. They haven't been damaged. I think that it's more important to keep up with the times. You can't stop change.

Protester: Can I interject something here?

Reporter: Here is the protester I was talking to before. He has more to say about the controversy. Go ahead, sir.

Protester: I totally disagree with what this shopper has to say. I'm protesting this store because I want to preserve our collective past, our cultural identity. The store will damage the spirit of this place. Is shopping more important than our heritage?

Reporter: But, sir. What about the local residents who need jobs? And don't shoppers have a right to buy items at a fair price in a store nearby?

Protester: Sure, but preserving this site is more important in the long run than the convenience of having a local superstore.

Reporter: Sir, what do you think about what the protester is saying?

Shopper: Well, we shouldn't knowingly destroy our heritage, but we do have to move forward with the rest of the world. We can't continue to live in the past. We need more modernization. Having a big store seems like progress to me.

Reporter: Well, as you can see, there is a conflict here in the Teotihuacán community between the need for jobs, low prices, and convenience and the desire to preserve the remains of one of Mexico's oldest and most impressive civilizations. Maybe the community will be able to reach some agreement. That's it for today from Teotihuacán.